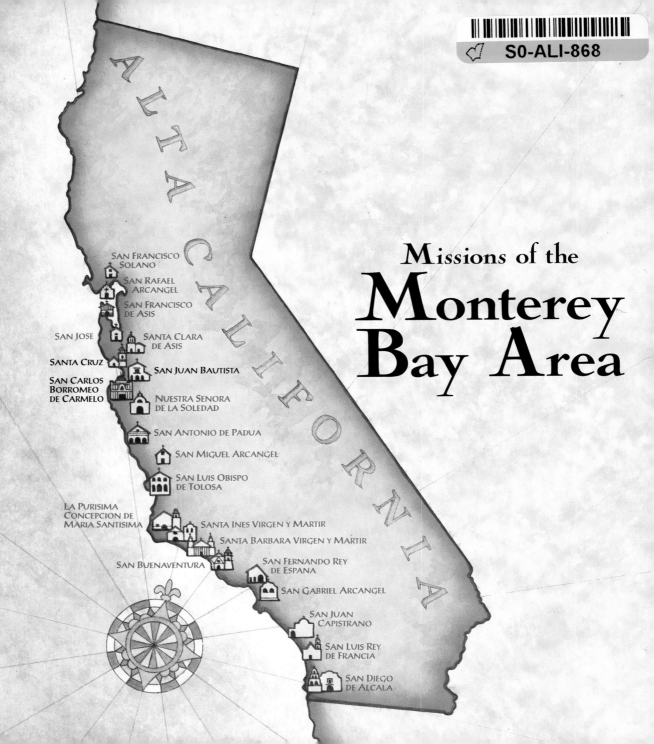

ALTA CALIFORNIA

Missions of the
Monterey
Bay Area

San Francisco Solano

San Rafael Arcangel

San Francisco de Asis

San Jose

Santa Clara de Asis

Santa Cruz

San Juan Bautista

San Carlos Borromeo de Carmelo

Nuestra Senora de la Soledad

San Antonio de Padua

San Miguel Arcangel

San Luis Obispo de Tolosa

La Purisima Concepcion de Maria Santisima

Santa Ines Virgen y Martir

Santa Barbara Virgen y Martir

San Buenaventura

San Fernando Rey de Espana

San Gabriel Arcangel

San Juan Capistrano

San Luis Rey de Francia

San Diego de Alcala

California MISSIONS

Missions of the
Monterey Bay Area

Emily Abbink

LERNER PUBLICATIONS COMPANY

Series editors: Karen Chernyaev, Mary M. Rodgers, Elizabeth Verdick
Series photo researcher: Amy Cox
Series designer: Zachary Marell

This book is available in two editions:
Library binding by Lerner Publications Company
Soft cover by First Avenue Editions, 1999.
241 First Avenue North
Minneapolis, MN 55401
ISBN: 0–8225–1928–3 (lib. bdg.)
ISBN: 0–8225–9835–3 (pbk.)

Website address: www.lernerbooks.com

LIBRARY OF CONGRESS CATALOGING-IN-PUBLICATION DATA

Abbink, Emily
    Missions of the Monterey Bay area / by Emily Abbink.
        p. cm. — (California Missions)
    Includes index.
    Summary: Charts the histories of the missions of Carmel, Santa Cruz, and San Juan Bautista, and briefly describes life among the Ohlone Indians before the arrival of the Spaniards.
        ISBN 0–8225–1928–3 (lib. bdg.)
    1. Spanish mission buildings—California—Monterey Bay Region—Juvenile literature.
    2. Monterey Bay Region (Calif.)—History—Juvenile literature. [1. Missions—California.
    2. California—History. 3. Costanoan Indians—Missions—California. 4. Indians of North America—Missions—California.] I. Title II. Series.
    F868.M7A23 1996
    979.4'76—dc20   95–2843

Manufactured in the United States of America
2 3 4 5 6 7 – JR – 03 02 01 00 99 98

Cover: **The old religious settlement of Mission San Carlos Borromeo features the Mudéjar Star window, an example of an architectural style once popular in Spain. Mudéjares were Muslims (followers of the Islamic faith) who lived in Spain after the 1200s.** *Title page:* **To reach the pulpit of the church at Mission San Juan Bautista, priests entered an elaborately decorated back stairway.**

This book is dedicated to the Ohlone peoples, past and present, of Monterey Bay and to Paul, Raphael, and Benny. The author also thanks Edna Kimbro, Randy Milliken, Karen Hildebrand, and Philip Laverty for their support and encouragement.

Every effort has been made to secure permission for the quoted material and for the photographs in this book.

CONTENTS

GLOSSARY / 6

PRONUNCIATION GUIDE / 7

PREFACE BY PROFESSOR EDWARD D. CASTILLO / 8

INTRODUCTION / 11

1 *Early Life along the Coast* / 17

2 *Missions of the Monterey Bay Area* / 29

Mission San Carlos Borromeo de Carmelo / 30

Mission Santa Cruz / 38

Mission San Juan Bautista / 46

3 *Secularization of the Missions* / 55

4 *The Missions in Modern Times* / 67

AFTERWORD BY DR. JAMES J. RAWLS / 74

CHRONOLOGY / 76

ACKNOWLEDGMENTS / 77

INDEX / 78

ABOUT THE AUTHOR AND THE CONSULTANTS / 80

GLOSSARY

adobe: A type of clay soil found in Mexico and in dry parts of the United States. In Alta California, workers formed wet adobe into bricks that hardened in the sun.

Alta California (Upper California): An old Spanish name for the present-day state of California.

Baja California (Lower California): A strip of land off the northwestern coast of Mexico that lies between the Pacific Ocean and the Gulf of California. Part of Mexico, Baja California borders the U.S. state of California.

Franciscan: A member of the Order of Friars Minor, a Roman Catholic community founded in Italy by Saint Francis of Assisi in 1209. The Franciscans are dedicated to performing missionary work and acts of charity.

mission: A center where missionaries (religious teachers) work to spread their beliefs to other people and to teach a new way of life.

missionary: A person sent out by a religious group to spread its beliefs to other people.

neophyte: A Greek word meaning "newly converted" that refers to an Indian baptized into the Roman Catholic community.

New Spain: A large area once belonging to Spain that included what are now the southwestern United States and Mexico. After 1821, when New Spain had gained its independence from the Spanish Empire, the region became known as the Republic of Mexico.

presidio: A Spanish fort for housing soldiers. In Alta California, Spaniards built presidios to protect the missions and priests from possible attacks and to enforce order in the region. California's four main presidios were located at San Diego, Santa Barbara, Monterey, and San Francisco.

quadrangle: A four-sided enclosure surrounded by buildings.

reservation: Tracts of land set aside by the U.S. government to be used by Native Americans.

secularization: A series of laws enacted by the Mexican government in the 1830s. The rulings aimed to take mission land and buildings from Franciscan control and to place the churches in the hands of parish priests, who didn't perform missionary work. Much of the land was distributed to families and individuals.

PRONUNCIATION GUIDE*

Branciforte	brahn-see-FOR-tay
Cabrillo, Juan Rodríguez	kah-BREE-yoh, WAHN roh-DREE-gays
Cuesta, Felipe del Arroyo de la	KWAYS-tah, fay-LEE-pay del ah-RO-yoh day lah
El Camino Reál	el kah-MEE-no ray-AHL
La Pérouse	lah pay-ROOZ
Lasuén, Fermín Francisco de	lah-soo-AYN, fair-MEEN frahn-SEES-koh day
Malaspina, Alejandro	mah-lah-SPEE-nah, ah-lay-HAHN-droh
Ohlone	oh-LOH-nee
Portolá, Gaspar de	por-toh-LAH, gahs-PAHR day
San Carlos Borromeo de Carmelo	SAHN KAR-lohs boh-roh-MAY-oh day kar-MAY-loh
San Juan Bautista	SAHN WAHN bahw-TEES-tah
Santa Cruz	SAHN-tah KROOS
Serra, Junípero	SEH-rrah, hoo-NEE-pay-roh
Tápis, Estéban	TAH-pees, ehs-TAY-bahn
Vizcaíno, Sebastián	vees-kah-EE-no, say-bahs-tee-AHN
Yokuts	YOH-kuhts

* Local pronunciations may differ.

PREFACE

The religious beliefs and traditions of the Indians of California teach that the blessings of a rich land and a mild climate are gifts from the Creator. The Indians show their love and respect for the Creator—and for all of creation—by carefully managing the land for future generations and by living in harmony with the natural environment.

Over the course of many centuries, the Indians of California organized small, independent societies. Only in the hot, dry deserts of southeastern California did they farm the land to feed themselves. Elsewhere, the abundance of fish, deer, antelope, waterfowl, and wild seeds supplied all that the Indians needed for survival. The economies of these societies did not create huge surpluses of food. Instead the people produced only what they expected would meet their needs. Yet there is no record of famine during the long period when Indians in California managed the land.

These age-old beliefs and practices stood in sharp contrast to the policies of the Spaniards who began to settle areas of California in the late 1700s. Spain established religious missions along the coast to anchor its empire in California. At these missions, Spanish priests baptized thousands of Indians into the Roman Catholic religion. Instead of continuing to hunt and gather their food, the Indians were made to work on mission estates where farming supported the settlements. Pastures for mission livestock soon took over Indian land, and European farming activities depleted native plants. Illnesses that the Spaniards had unintentionally carried from Europe brought additional suffering to many Indian groups.

The Indians living in California numbered 340,000 in the late 1700s, but only 100,000 remained after roughly 70 years of Spanish missionization. Many of the Indians died from disease. Spanish soldiers killed other Indians during native revolts at the missions. Some entire Indian societies were wiped out.

Thousands of mission Indian descendants proudly continue to practice their native culture and to speak their native language. But what is most important to these survivors is that their people's history be understood by those who now call California home, as well as by others across the nation. Through this series of books, young readers will learn for the first time how the missions affected the Indians and their traditional societies.

Perhaps one of the key lessons to be learned from an honest and evenhanded account of California's missions is that the Indians had something important to teach the Spaniards and the people who came to the region later. Our ancestors and today's elders instill in us that we must respect and live in harmony with animals, plants, and one another. While this is an ancient wisdom, it seems especially relevant to our future survival.

Professor Edward D. Castillo
Cahuilla-Luiseño Mission Indian Descendant

INTRODUCTION

FOUNDED BY SPAIN, THE CALIFORNIA **MISSIONS** ARE located on a narrow strip of California's Pacific coast. Some of the historic buildings sit near present-day Highway 101, which roughly follows what was once a roadway called El Camino Reál (the Royal Road), so named to honor the king of Spain. The trail linked a chain of 21 missions set up between 1769 and 1823.

Spain, along with leaders of the Roman Catholic Church, established missions and *presidios* (forts) throughout the Spanish Empire to strengthen its claim to the land. In the 1600s, Spain built mission settlements on the peninsula known as **Baja California,** as well as in other areas of **New Spain** (present-day Mexico).

The goal of the Spanish mission system in North America was to make Indians accept Spanish ways and become loyal subjects of the Spanish king. Priests functioning as **missionaries** (religious teachers) tried to convert the local Indian populations to Catholicism and to

In the mid-1700s, Native Americans living in what is now California came into contact with Roman Catholic missionaries from Spain.

teach them to dress and behave like Spaniards. Soldiers came to protect the missionaries and to make sure the Indians obeyed the priests.

During the late 1700s, Spain wanted to spread its authority northward from Baja California into the region known as **Alta California,** where Spain's settlement pattern would be repeated. The first group of Spanish soldiers and missionaries traveled to Alta California in 1769. The missionaries, priests of the **Franciscan** order, were led by Junípero Serra, the father-president of the mission system.

The soldiers and missionaries came into contact with communities of Native Americans, or Indians, that dotted the coastal and inland areas of Alta California. For thousands of years, the region had been home to many Native American groups that spoke a wide variety of languages. Using these Indians as unpaid laborers was vital to the success of the mission system. The mission economy was based on agriculture—a way of life unfamiliar to local Indians, who mostly hunted game and gathered wild plants for food.

Although some Indians willingly joined the missions, the Franciscans relied on various methods to convince or force other Native Americans to become part of the mission system. The priests sometimes lured Indians with gifts of glass beads and colored cloth or other items new to the Native Americans. Some Indians who lost their hunting and food-gathering grounds to mission farms and ranches joined the Spanish settlements to survive. In other cases, Spanish soldiers forcibly took villagers from their homes.

Neophytes, or Indians recruited into the missions, were expected to learn the Catholic faith and the skills for farming and building. Afterward—Spain reasoned—the Native Americans would be able to manage the property themselves, a process that officials figured would take 10 years. But a much different turn of events took place.

Some cemeteries at the missions hold the remains of neophytes (baptized Indians). The tomb of Old Gabriel stands in the cemetery of Mission San Carlos, also known as Carmel.

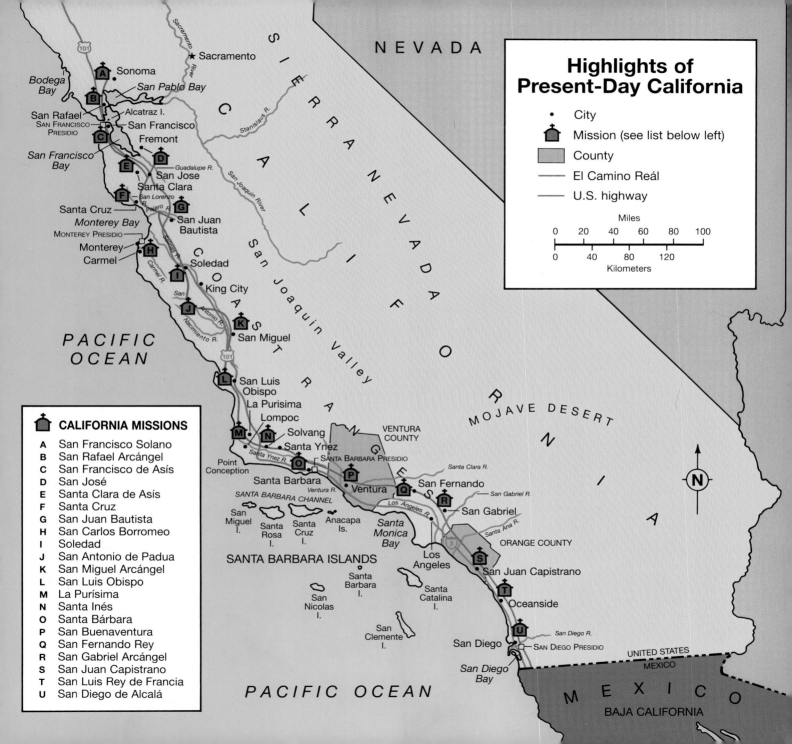

PACIFIC OCEAN

NEVADA

Highlights of Present-Day California

- • City
- 🏛 Mission (see list below left)
- ▢ County
- ── El Camino Reál
- ── U.S. highway

Miles
0   20   40   60   80   100

0   40   80   120
Kilometers

🏛 CALIFORNIA MISSIONS

A   San Francisco Solano
B   San Rafael Arcángel
C   San Francisco de Asís
D   San José
E   Santa Clara de Asís
F   Santa Cruz
G   San Juan Bautista
H   San Carlos Borromeo
I   Soledad
J   San Antonio de Padua
K   San Miguel Arcángel
L   San Luis Obispo
M   La Purísima
N   Santa Inés
O   Santa Bárbara
P   San Buenaventura
Q   San Fernando Rey
R   San Gabriel Arcángel
S   San Juan Capistrano
T   San Luis Rey de Francia
U   San Diego de Alcalá

Sacramento River

Bodega Bay
Sonoma
San Pablo Bay
San Rafael
SAN FRANCISCO PRESIDIO
Alcatraz I.
San Francisco
San Francisco Bay
Fremont
Guadalupe R.
San Jose
Santa Clara
Santa Cruz
San Lorenzo R.
Pajaro R.
San Juan Bautista
Monterey Bay
MONTEREY PRESIDIO
Monterey
Carmel
Carmel R.
Soledad
Salinas R.
San
King City
Antonio R.
San Miguel
Nacimiento R.

SIERRA NEVADA

Stanislaus R.
San Joaquin River
San Joaquin Valley

COAST RANGE

★ Sacramento

San Luis Obispo
La Purísima
Lompoc
Solvang
Santa Ynez
Point Conception
Santa Ynez R.
SANTA BARBARA PRESIDIO
Santa Barbara
Ventura R.
Ventura

VENTURA COUNTY

MOJAVE DESERT

Santa Clara R.
San Fernando
Los Angeles R.
San Gabriel R.
San Gabriel
ORANGE COUNTY
Santa Ana R.
Los Angeles
San Juan Capistrano
Oceanside
San Diego R.
San Diego
SAN DIEGO PRESIDIO
San Diego Bay

SANTA BARBARA CHANNEL
San Miguel I.
Santa Rosa I.
Santa Cruz I.
Anacapa Is.
Santa Monica Bay
SANTA BARBARA ISLANDS
Santa Barbara I.
San Nicolas I.
San Clemente I.
Santa Catalina I.

UNITED STATES
MEXICO
MEXICO
BAJA CALIFORNIA

PACIFIC OCEAN

N

California Mission	Founding Date
San Diego de Alcalá	July 16, 1769
San Carlos Borromeo de Carmelo	June 3, 1770
San Antonio de Padua	July 14, 1771
San Gabriel Arcángel	September 8, 1771
San Luis Obispo de Tolosa	September 1, 1772
San Francisco de Asís	June 29, 1776
San Juan Capistrano	November 1, 1776
Santa Clara de Asís	January 12, 1777
San Buenaventura	March 31, 1782
Santa Bárbara Virgen y Mártir	December 4, 1786
La Purísima Concepción de Maria Santísima	December 8, 1787
Santa Cruz	August 28, 1791
Nuestra Señora de la Soledad	October 9, 1791
San José	June 11, 1797
San Juan Bautista	June 24, 1797
San Miguel Arcángel	July 25, 1797
San Fernando Rey de España	September 8, 1797
San Luis Rey de Francia	June 13, 1798
Santa Inés Virgen y Mártir	September 17, 1804
San Rafael Arcángel	December 14, 1817
San Francisco Solano	July 4, 1823

Forced to abandon their villages and to give up their age-old traditions, many Native Americans didn't adjust to mission life. In fact, most Indians died soon after entering the missions—mainly from European diseases that eventually killed thousands of Indians throughout California.

Because hundreds of Indian laborers worked at each mission, most of the settlements thrived. The missions produced grapes, olives, wheat, cattle hides, cloth, soap, candles, and other goods. In fact, the missions successfully introduced to Alta California a variety of crops and livestock that still benefit present-day Californians.

The missions became so productive that the Franciscans established a valuable trade network. Mission priests exchanged goods and provided nearby soldiers and settlers with provisions. The agricultural wealth of the missions angered many set-

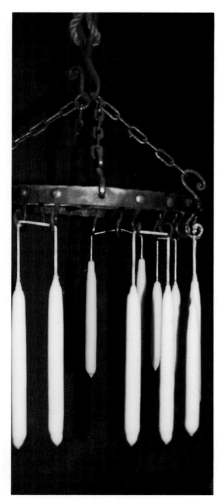

To make candles, mission Indians dipped strings in hot tallow (animal fat) over and over again until a thick coating of wax built up.

tlers and soldiers, who resented the priests for holding Alta California's most fertile land and the majority of the livestock and for controlling the Indian labor force.

This resentment grew stronger after 1821, when New Spain became the independent country of Mexico. Mexico claimed Alta California and began the **secularization** of the missions. The mission churches still offered religious services, but the Spanish Franciscans were to be replaced by secular priests. These priests weren't missionaries seeking to convert people.

By 1836 the neophytes were free to leave the missions, and the settlements quickly declined from the loss of workers. Few of the former neophytes found success away from the missions, however. Many continued as forced laborers on *ranchos* (ranches) or in nearby *pueblos* (towns), earning little or no pay.

In 1848 Mexico lost a war against the United States and ceded Alta California to the U.S. government. By that time, about half of Alta California's Indian population had died. Neophytes who had remained at the missions often had no village to which to return. They moved to pueblos or to inland areas. Meanwhile, the missions went into a state of decay, only to be rebuilt years later.

This book covers the history and current conditions of the three missions located in the area around Monterey Bay. Founded in 1770, San Carlos Borromeo de Carmelo, the headquarters of the father-presidents, was the second mission of the chain. Santa Cruz, the twelfth mission, was established on the opposite side of the bay 21 years later. In 1797 the Franciscans set up the fifteenth mission—San Juan Bautista. Ohlone Indians made up most of the neophyte population at these three missions, but members of inland tribes also became laborers.

PART ONE

Early Life along the Coast

THE CHILLY WATERS OF MONTEREY BAY, ON CALIfornia's Pacific coast, churn continuously. Mussels and abalones cling to the underwater rocks. These shellfish and other small sea creatures thrive on the continuous upwelling of rich food. Countless otters, seals, sharks, and birds feed on the abundant water life.

An incoming wave sprays salt water and foam over the rocky landscape of Monterey Bay, where abalones (top inset) and sea lions (bottom inset) live. At one time, Ohlone Indians thrived on the rich food supply available in the bay area.

The Carmel, Salinas, Pajaro, and San Lorenzo rivers all drain into Monterey Bay from the nearby Coast Ranges. These rivers water grassy valleys that flood with winter rains to form vast, foggy wetlands such as

The Pajaro River flows into Monterey Bay. The river's name comes from the Spanish word for a feathered bird.

Clumps of tule reeds offered the Ohlone plentiful raw materials for making boats. The Indians dried the reeds and then tied them into thick bundles.

Elkhorn Slough. The valleys and wetlands provide homes for many kinds of animals. Acres of tules and other marsh grasses grow here, too.

For the Ohlone Indians, whose villages once ringed the shore of Monterey Bay, the area was rich and diverse with native flora and fauna. Vast redwood forests and miles of grasslands covered the mountain slopes. Acorns, *piñon* nuts, berries, and wild roots were plentiful.

Grizzly bears and mountain lions stalked deer, elk, and ante-

Among the world's tallest trees, coast redwoods get moisture from the fog that rolls off the Pacific Ocean.

lope across the mountains and meadows. Great flocks of wild geese and ducks darkened the sky with their numbers. Trout and salmon packed the rivers. Millions of smelt crowded the beaches. Whales often spouted close offshore.

For hundreds of years, the Ohlone of Monterey Bay were part of this environmental richness. The abundance and variety of plant and animal foods allowed the people to live in the bay area year-round.

Native American Life

Indians may have first arrived in North America several thousand years ago. Some groups eventually settled in California's deserts, mountains, and valleys and along the Pacific coast.

About 40 Ohlone tribelets (small village-states) formed along the coast. A tribelet was usually made up of several villages. Tribelets numbered

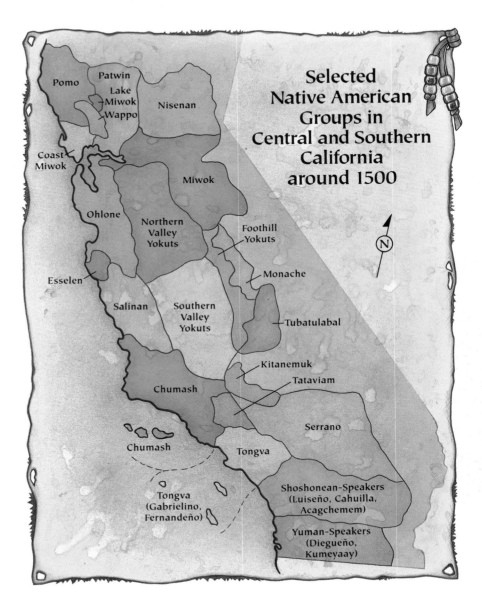

Selected Native American Groups in Central and Southern California around 1500

Pomo
Patwin
Lake Miwok
Wappo
Nisenan
Coast Miwok
Miwok
Ohlone
Northern Valley Yokuts
Foothill Yokuts
Monache
Esselen
Salinan
Southern Valley Yokuts
Tubatulabal
Kitanemuk
Tataviam
Chumash
Serrano
Chumash
Tongva
Tongva (Gabrielino, Fernandeño)
Shoshonean-Speakers (Luiseño, Cahuilla, Acagchemem)
Yuman-Speakers (Diegueño, Kumeyaay)

N

The Ohlone ate a variety of wild fruits, including grapes, that grew through-out their territory.

The Ohlone were not farmers, but they did practice some kinds of agriculture. For example, the people set fire to small sections of grassland. The fire destroyed old, seedless growth and made room for new, seed-producing plants to spring up and thrive. By providing space to the young shoots, the Ohlone were able to gather more seeds at harvesttime.

between 100 and 500 people, with an average of 250 villagers. Among the tribelets, eight to twelve different but related languages were spoken.

Every season the people moved within their tribal territories to hunt, to fish, or to harvest wild plants. They crossed tribelet boundaries when invited to attend ceremonies, to harvest with relatives, and to trade.

Each tribelet had either a man or a woman as chief. Tribelet chiefs fed visitors, provided for the needy, settled disputes, directed ceremonies, and advised villagers. With a council of elders, the chiefs also organized hunting, fishing, gathering, and warring expeditions.

The Ohlone groups didn't raise crops. Instead, the Native Americans gathered wild plant foods. Villagers harvested local seeds, acorns, berries, and roots. The Native Americans dried and stored these foods for use throughout the year.

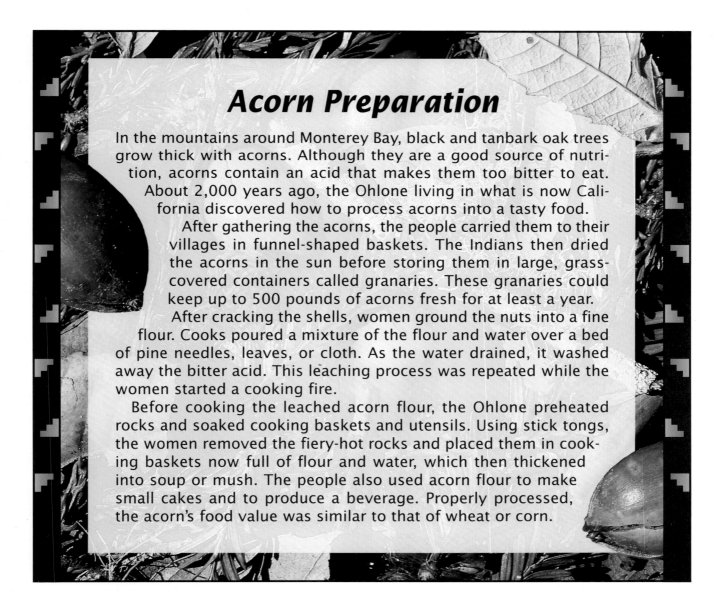

Acorn Preparation

In the mountains around Monterey Bay, black and tanbark oak trees grow thick with acorns. Although they are a good source of nutrition, acorns contain an acid that makes them too bitter to eat. About 2,000 years ago, the Ohlone living in what is now California discovered how to process acorns into a tasty food.

After gathering the acorns, the people carried them to their villages in funnel-shaped baskets. The Indians then dried the acorns in the sun before storing them in large, grass-covered containers called granaries. These granaries could keep up to 500 pounds of acorns fresh for at least a year.

After cracking the shells, women ground the nuts into a fine flour. Cooks poured a mixture of the flour and water over a bed of pine needles, leaves, or cloth. As the water drained, it washed away the bitter acid. This leaching process was repeated while the women started a cooking fire.

Before cooking the leached acorn flour, the Ohlone preheated rocks and soaked cooking baskets and utensils. Using stick tongs, the women removed the fiery-hot rocks and placed them in cooking baskets now full of flour and water, which then thickened into soup or mush. The people also used acorn flour to make small cakes and to produce a beverage. Properly processed, the acorn's food value was similar to that of wheat or corn.

A drawing from the 1800s shows how Indians in California speared fish from shallow waters.

The Ohlone used spears, bows and arrows, nets, and snares to hunt deer, rabbits, water birds, salmon, and marine animals. Along the shore, the Native Americans gathered shellfish, netted smelt, and oc- casionally butchered beached whales.

The Ohlone Indians made knives, hammers, and weapons from wood, bone, and stone. The Indians wove lightweight mats, blankets, cords, baby car- riers, clothing, and nets from cattails and other strong marsh grasses. The Ohlone also fash- ioned boats by tying bundles of tules together.

Some of the people moved seasonally in search of food. Wherever the Ohlone relocated, they built tule dwellings. To make the homes, the Indians thatched grass over and around a framework of poles. This sort of house could be closed or left open to the weather. In addi- tion, villagers could build the structures quickly.

Ohlone men and boys wore few clothes in the bay's warm climate. The women and girls wore hide-and-grass skirts and in cold weather used deerskin capes.

This late-eighteenth-century image depicts an Ohlone woman from the Monterey area clothed in a grass skirt and a cape made from an animal skin.

The dome-shaped homes of Ohlone Indians were simple to put up. Because the people could relocate easily, they were free to search for food from season to season.

The Ohlone occasionally fought with non-Ohlone peoples and sometimes sparred with other Ohlone tribelets. Hostilities were especially fierce between the Rumsien Ohlone, who lived near the Carmel River, and the Esselen and Salinan tribes to the south. Most fighting was to defend or challenge access to certain trade routes or hunting and gathering areas.

Coastal Ohlone groups often traded shells, dried shellfish, and obsidian (black volcanic glass) to inland peoples. In exchange the Ohlone received arrowheads, piñon nuts, stone and bone beads, and chert (rock) for tools. Everyone prized cinnabar (a metallic ore) from the nearby Santa Cruz Mountains for its use as a red body paint important in ceremonial activities.

The coastal Ohlone also crafted money from olivella shells. The Indians collected the tiny spiral shells and ground off the tips to form an opening for stringing the beads onto a cord. People used strands of this shell-bead money to buy food from other groups in times of need.

Ohlone religion affected almost every part of the group's lifestyle. Religious beliefs centered around creating harmony and balance by treating the natural environment as sacred. For example, hunting, gathering, cooking, basketmaking, and many other activities all called for special prayers or rituals of thanks. The people prayed daily to the sun with offerings of seeds, tobacco leaves, shell beads, and woven capes.

Even dancing was a form of prayer. Dancers often tried to create harmony between people and spirits. Sometimes villagers danced to tell a story. Split-stick clappers and bone whistles accompanied singers and dancers. Seedpod and cocoon rattles shook with each step.

Shamans were the Ohlone religious leaders. Male and female shamans tried to heal the sick with singing, dancing, and

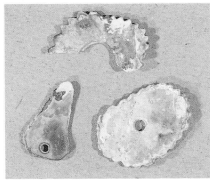

Ohlone craftspeople punched holes in delicate shells (above) *and strung the ornaments into jewelry. Ohlone shamans* (left) *wore shells, animal teeth, rocks, and other items during ceremonies and celebrations.*

Work, fun, and rest made up a typical day in an Ohlone village. Children played games under the watchful eye of women who soaked grasses to make baskets or who tended small cooking fires. The women also hung meat to dry in the sun, while men hunted or gathered wood.

herbs. The shamans prayed for good harvests, for successful hunts, and, when needed, for a change in the weather.

European Contact

In the 1500s, Spaniards came to Alta California's Pacific coast looking for safe harbors, gold, and a waterway connecting the Atlantic and Pacific Oceans. Because the Ohlone lived around Monterey Bay—a natural harbor for ships—they were among the first of the region's Indians to meet European explorers.

In 1542 the Portuguese-born explorer Juan Rodríguez Cabrillo probably became the first European to see Monterey Bay. Although stormy seas prevented him from landing in the bay area, he claimed the region for Spain.

In 1602 Sebastián Vizcaíno explored the Monterey coast by ship for the Spanish king. The explorer mapped the bay and described it as an excellent harbor. Vizcaíno's notes mention that the Rumsien Ohlone from the south bay were good natured and generous. They brought the European sailors the skins of mountain lions, bears, and deer and offered the newcomers shellfish to eat.

For the next 160 years, Spain paid little attention to Alta California. But in the mid-1700s, Spanish officials suspected that England and Russia wanted to conquer the area. This threat encouraged Spain to act.

One way Spain could try to secure its loose claim to Alta California—a claim recognized only by other European nations—was to send people there to live. But few Spaniards were willing to settle in faraway Alta California. So Spain decided to do what it had done elsewhere in the world—build missions. At these religious settlements, Franciscan priests would teach the local Native Americans how to become Spanish-speaking, Catholic citizens. Officials expected the Indians to be loyal to the Spanish king.

In 1769 Captain Gaspar de Portolá led the first land expedition from New Spain to Alta California. In that same year, he helped to set up San Diego de Alcalá, the first mission in the region.

"WEEPING AND SHOUTING IN FEAR, THE VILLAGERS BROUGHT GASPAR DE PORTOLÁ'S SOLDIERS SEEDCAKES TO EAT, HOPING THE STRANGERS WOULD GO AWAY."

Spain also wanted to build a mission and a presidio at Monterey Bay. Using Vizcaíno's map, Portolá and his group of soldiers rode northward on horseback from what is now the city of San Diego. But when Portolá finally reached Monterey Bay, he didn't recognize it. Vizcaíno's notes, written from his ship, described a sea view rather than a land view of the region. Vizcaíno had also exaggerated the value of the bay as a harbor.

Not aware that they had already reached Vizcaíno's bay, Portolá's soldiers galloped northward along the shore and came upon a large Ohlone village. The gun-carrying Spaniards, their armor shining, seemed to appear out of nowhere.

The terrified Ohlone believed that rider and horse were one monstrous animal. Weeping and shouting in fear, the villagers brought the soldiers seedcakes to eat, hoping the strangers would go away. Portolá's men gave the Ohlone glass beads and continued north, looking for Monterey Bay.

Two days later, the Spaniards returned. To their surprise, they found the Ohlone village abandoned and burned to the ground. The Spaniards named the area Pajaro, after a large, straw-stuffed bird left fastened to the top of a pole. Portolá's exploration party then went back to San Diego, believing they hadn't found Monterey Bay.

Within a year, sailors on Spanish supply ships recognized Vizcaíno's bay from the sea. These people informed Portolá, now on a second land expedition, that he'd reached Monterey on his first trip.

The ships were bringing supplies to Junípero Serra, father-president of the missions in Alta California. At Monterey Bay, Serra and Spanish military leaders intended to set up a mission and a presidio. Portolá's troops camped at the mouth of the Carmel River, looking for a good place to build the Spanish settlements. One evening the Spaniards saw many unarmed Rumsien Ohlone silently watching the Spanish camp. About 40 Rumsien then came forward carrying feather-tipped poles and baskets of seed flour as peace offerings.

In return Portolá gave the Ohlone beads and ribbons. The chief, walking ahead of the others, was painted shiny black. He promised to bring venison (deer meat) in four days, which he did. The chief most likely hoped these strangers would leave soon.

The Spaniards were there to stay, however. In 1770 they built Mission San Carlos Borromeo de Carmelo and the Presidio of Monterey on the southern shore of the bay.

Using the shipboard records of an earlier European explorer, Captain Gaspar de Portolá traveled overland to reach the Monterey Bay area. He didn't recognize the bay at first because his notes described the bay from a sea view, which didn't match the view he had from land.

PART TWO

Missions of the Monterey Bay Area

INTO THE OHLONE WORLD OF STABILITY, TRADITION, and harmony with nature came the Spaniards. San Carlos Borromeo de Carmelo was the first of seven missions founded in Ohlone territory. Three of these missions were located near Monterey Bay.

The three missions founded around Monterey Bay shared many features, yet their individual histories are unique. Mission San

The setting sun bathes Mission San Juan Bautista in pink light. The mission was named for Saint John the Baptist, a cousin of Jesus, who urged people to prepare for Jesus' coming.

Carlos Borromeo de Carmelo, also called Carmel, was Father Serra's headquarters. Because the head of the missions lived at Carmel, it and the nearby presidio became the seat of Alta California's government.

While Mission San Carlos did fairly well, Mission Santa Cruz seemed destined to struggle from the beginning. Several missionaries, as well as many of the Indian laborers, did not seem to like the place. Later, a nearby settlement of Spanish-speakers, jealous of the mission's wealth, interfered with the Franciscans' ability to run Santa Cruz. Mission San Juan Bautista, on the other hand, was among the most productive of the 21 missions eventually established along El Camino Reál.

Mission San Carlos Borromeo de Carmelo

Soon after founding San Carlos Borromeo, Father Serra moved the mission south to the Carmel River. This spot was closer to the Rumsien village of Ashista and farther from the Presidio of Monterey.

From his headquarters, Father Serra began to plan the mission chain. He wrote guidelines explaining what methods the missionaries should use to convince Native Americans to join the missions. Through letters, he recruited Franciscans from Spain. Ships from Europe stopped at Carmel to visit with this energetic, determined priest.

Curiosity attracted many Native Americans to Carmel at first. The Indians liked the music and vestments (ceremonial robes) that the priests used during church services. Many Ohlone hoped to get guns,

Cowboys at San Carlos marked the mission's horses and cattle with this brand.

Junípero Serra

Father Junípero Serra was born Miguel José Serra in 1713 on the Spanish island of Majorca. As a boy, he enjoyed visiting the Roman Catholic priests at the little church near his home. Serra began his formal religious training at age 15, and by the time he was 18 he had become a priest in the Franciscan religious order. At that time, Father Serra changed

A modern statue of Father Serra stands at Carmel.

his first name to Junípero, after the faithful companion of Saint Francis of Assisi, founder of the order.

Serra felt that being a missionary was a priest's most meaningful role. Franciscan missionaries tried to convince nonbelievers to choose the Catholic faith by exposing them to Catholic teachings. The Catholic Church regarded its beliefs as the only ones worth following. It sent missionaries to non-Christian parts of the world, including Alta California.

Father Serra firmly believed in the teachings of the Bible and in one God. While in Alta California, he dreamed of baptizing all the Indians. Father Serra sincerely felt that his missionary activities would benefit the Indians. Despite poor health, quarrels with governors, and lack of supplies, Serra worked hard to realize his goal before his death in 1784.

horses, or other European items. Other villagers wanted to capture the strong spiritual power the Franciscans seemed to have.

Mission Life

Before Indians joined a mission, however, they had to go through baptism. During this religious ritual, water is poured over the head, welcoming a person into the Roman Catholic community. Baptized Indians became known as neophytes.

Soon the neophytes were required to move to the mission, where they had to make many changes. The Indians began to wear European-style clothes and to learn prayers in Latin, the language of the Catholic Church. The Franciscans taught the neophytes to farm and to herd livestock.

Attracting skilled workers to remote parts of the Spanish Empire, such as Alta California, was difficult. With guidebooks but often little training, Franciscans and neophytes constructed most of the mission buildings. These *adobe* (mud-brick) structures were practical and simple.

At Carmel the Franciscans and neophytes built a small

Dating to about 1800, this drawing of Mission San Carlos includes the Mudéjar Star window.

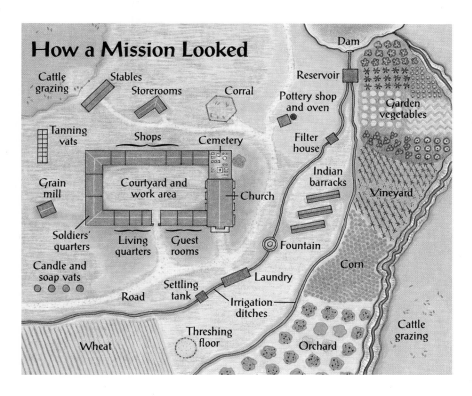

How a Mission Looked

Cattle grazing
Stables
Storerooms
Corral
Dam
Reservoir
Pottery shop and oven
Garden vegetables
Tanning vats
Shops
Cemetery
Filter house
Grain mill
Courtyard and work area
Church
Indian barracks
Vineyard
Soldiers' quarters
Living quarters
Guest rooms
Fountain
Candle and soap vats
Laundry
Corn
Settling tank
Road
Irrigation ditches
Cattle grazing
Threshing floor
Wheat
Orchard

The Franciscans used the same layout for most of the missions they founded in Alta California. A four-sided area, or quadrangle, was the hub of outer storerooms, workrooms, gardens, and pastures.

church, living quarters for the priests, soldiers' barracks, and a *monjerio* (home for young, unmarried female neophytes). Other buildings included a kitchen, stables, workshops, and a granary. The structures surrounded a large, open plaza where people could gather. This four-sided design was known as a **quadrangle.** The neophytes built traditional tule dwellings outside the quadrangle, where married neophytes lived after their children had been removed to live inside the mission. Eventually, this village of tule dwellings grew quite large.

Mission San Carlos was something like a school but with several big differences. The neophytes had to live at the mission and couldn't leave. If the Indians tried to leave the mission and return to their old way of life, Spanish soldiers brought them back. The neophytes had to work much harder and longer than they were used to. And they were punished, often harshly, for disobeying. Father Serra favored strong punishment, believing the neophytes would learn faster. He also thought that hard work, suffering, and dedication were necessary to become a good Catholic.

Mission San Carlos Borromeo de Carmelo was named after Carlo Borromeo, a reform-minded leader of the Roman Catholic Church who lived in Milan, Italy, in the 1500s. The mission's church *(left)* is the only one among the 21 settlements that still has a dome. The church's interior *(below left)* contains many statues. In another part of the compound is a monument to Father Serra *(above)*.

The neophytes were kept busy making necessities for Mission San Carlos. The neophytes worked as potters, weavers, seamstresses, cooks, candle and soap makers, adobe builders, carpenters, and blacksmiths. The Indians washed clothes, made boots and harnesses, and tanned leather.

Despite success in making some products, food crops took time to develop. Meanwhile, Father Serra expected the neophytes to give up their traditional foods and to eat wheat and corn made according to Spanish recipes.

Sometimes the Franciscans couldn't provide enough food for the neophytes. Crops occasionally failed because the region was too foggy for growing wheat and barley. During the winter of 1773 to 1774, meals consisted of ground peas and milk. The neophytes often had to rely on their hunting and gathering skills to survive.

Eventually, the priests improved their growing methods, and crops began to do well in the climate at Carmel. But the many fields took up Ohlone territory, leaving the Indians with no place to hunt and gather. By 1780 most of the nearby villagers had little choice but to move to Mission San Carlos.

THE FRENCH NOBLE LA PÉROUSE VISITED CARMEL IN *1786* AND WROTE THAT THE MISSIONARIES THERE WERE "PIOUS, PRUDENT, HOSPITABLE, AND DEVOTED."

Visitors to Carmel

In 1784 Father Serra died. One year later, the Catholic Church appointed Father Fermín Francisco de Lasuén to replace Serra as father-president. Father Lasuén also used Carmel as his headquarters. Although the loss of Father Serra saddened the Franciscans, the missions continued to function. In fact, Mission San Carlos produced enough goods to support the priests, the neophytes, and the soldiers and to trade with other missions.

Spain wouldn't allow settlements in Alta California to trade with non-Spanish merchants, and foreign visitors rarely came by land. As a result, the Franciscans entertained few outsiders.

So it was thrilling when French explorer Jean-François de Galaup, Count of La Pérouse, sailed into Monterey Bay in 1786. His were the first non-Spanish ships legally allowed to visit the Franciscans in Alta California. The king of Spain commanded Mission San Carlos

The Journey of a Journal

Mission San Carlos was only one of many stops for the French explorer La Pérouse. In 1785 he began a long voyage throughout the Pacific in search of trade and scientific information. During his years away from France, he took careful notes of his findings and adventures. His travels took him to North America, Asia, and the South Pacific.

In 1787, during his stay in northeastern Asia, La Pérouse mailed his journal to France for safekeeping. His writings included detailed observations of the neophytes at Mission San Carlos. A year later, La Pérouse and his crew were seen leaving Australia. They were never heard from again.

In the early 1800s, a British captain found evidence that suggested La Pérouse and his crew had been killed by native peoples of the Solomon Islands, just east of Australia. Had La Pérouse kept his journal with him, some valuable insights into mission life would have been lost forever.

Neophytes and priests greeted the arrival of La Pérouse, who later recorded his thoughts of San Carlos in a journal.

Borromeo to welcome and assist La Pérouse.

La Pérouse and his men were in Alta California on a research expedition. During their 10-day visit at Carmel—their only stop in Alta California—the Frenchmen recorded information about the animals, climate, and geography of Monterey Bay. The scientists collected plants and made maps. La Pérouse had a favorable view of Monterey Bay's natural wealth and beauty. He wrote, "No country is more abundant in fish and game of every description."

The group's notes and illustrations also described the Ohlone and life at Carmel. La Pérouse found fault with Mission San Carlos de Carmelo. He said the settlement resembled slave plantations (large farms), where the workers had no rights or freedoms. La Pérouse believed that the Spanish missions were outdated. France, he reasoned, was far more deserving of

The Spanish naval commander Alejandro Malaspina (above) charted Monterey Bay while living at the presidio (fort) in nearby Monterey.

Alta California's natural riches than Spain was.

Commander Alejandro Malaspina, the next important visitor to drop anchor in Monterey Bay, took a different view of the missions. Malaspina was heading a Spanish scientific expedition along the Pacific

coast. By 1791 Malaspina had mapped Canada's western shore. He then sailed south to Monterey to gather supplies, to give his crew a break, and to record information.

The neophytes at Carmel, for example, helped Malaspina to assemble a vocabulary of Rumsien words, recording the language for the first time. The scientists collected plants, animals, rocks, and artifacts. Like La Pérouse, Malaspina kept a journal of his travels. In it Malaspina, whose trip was funded by Spain, promoted the founding of Spanish missions in Alta California.

Captain George Vancouver from Britain visited Carmel in 1793. He was interested in the northern fur trade. Like Malaspina, Vancouver had also mapped the Pacific coastline of what are now Canada and Washington State.

Vancouver stayed at Carmel during the construction of a

stone church designed by Manuel Ruíz, a master stonemason from New Spain. The mission's community had been growing, and the Franciscans saw a need for a bigger church. In 1793 Ruíz drew up impressive plans that took the neophytes four years to complete. The building featured sandstone block, adobe, burned brick, wooden beams, and floor and roof tiles.

During construction Vancouver presented Father Lasuén with a church organ. Illustrators from Vancouver's expedition sketched the mission and new church foundations. Like La Pérouse, Vancouver had much to say about the backwardness of Alta California's mission system. Vancouver described Carmel as uncivilized, lonely, and wretched. In his opinion, Alta California could be uplifted only under British control. Despite these foreign reports, Alta California remained under Spanish influence with Carmel and the Presidio of Monterey as the hub of the region.

Mission Santa Cruz

In 1769, during Gaspar de Portolá's expedition, the explorer traveled to a fertile plain on Monterey Bay's northern shore, near the San Lorenzo River. He named the area Santa Cruz (Holy Cross). Years later, on August 28, 1791, Father Lasuén raised a large cross on the region named by Portolá. The cross marked the location for the twelfth mission.

To help Mission Santa Cruz get started, nearby Mission Santa Clara sent Indian workers and supplied horses, cattle, bread, and seeds. The Presidio of San Francisco donated oxen, sheep, and barley.

The iron brand, or hierro, *of Mission Santa Cruz labeled the mission's livestock.*

The Presidio of Monterey was the main outpost for the missions of the Monterey Bay area. The fortress was outfitted with large barracks and observation points.

The Franciscans soon moved Mission Santa Cruz uphill to escape flooding from the San Lorenzo River. This new location was also closer to a large Ohlone village, possibly called Uyipi, where tule dwellings overlooked the bay.

The new mission had a promising future, with a good climate, fertile soil, plentiful water, and peaceful Indians. Soon large herds of cattle and sheep grazed the coastal pastures, and crops lined the riverbanks. In 1794 neophytes finished a stone and adobe church. They built the rest of the quadrangle afterward.

Many of the Indians who came to Mission Santa Cruz were curious about the Roman Catholic religion. Some Native Americans feared the Franciscans, believing the priests had the power to make villagers sick if they didn't join the mission. Still others came for gifts, food, and protection from enemy tribes.

The first neophytes at Santa Cruz worked at the mission and attended church but were allowed to live in their villages. The villages were nearby, so the neophytes could easily hear the mission bells, which called the people to work or church services.

In 1797 Mission Santa Cruz began to have some serious trouble. That year the governor of Alta California established Branciforte, a pueblo on the east bank of the San Lorenzo River. The Franciscans protested that the town was too close to the mission. They were afraid the townspeople, later called Californios, would let their livestock take over mission pastures. More importantly, the priests didn't want outsiders, many of whom were not churchgoers, setting bad examples for the neophytes.

Nevertheless, the Californios arrived in Branciforte—without seeds, livestock, tools, or building supplies. The settlers expected the mission's laborers to build the town's homes and to provide necessities until the newcomers got settled.

Branciforte, however, failed miserably. The people were jealous of the vast mission herds and croplands and wanted an unpaid Indian workforce of their own. The Californios stole mission produce and livestock and demanded work from the neophytes. The missionaries at Santa Cruz refused to keep helping the townspeople, and tensions grew.

Highlights of Monterey Bay Area, early 1800s

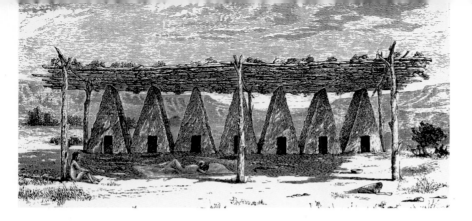

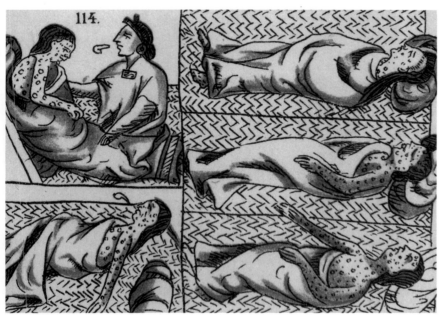

(Top) An old drawing shows the pointed dwellings of the Yokuts Indians whom the missionaries recruited into Santa Cruz. (Bottom) Many of these Indians—as well as the original Ohlone neophytes—died of European diseases to which they had no resistance. This illustration depicts the suffering of victims of smallpox, a sickness that spreads easily from person to person through the air.

Disease and Medicine

Like many mission Indians, the neophytes at Santa Cruz suffered terribly from deadly diseases the Spaniards brought from Europe. Measles, smallpox, scarlet fever, cholera, and influenza were sicknesses new to the California Indians, and they had no resistance. By the early 1800s, the local population of Ohlone had dropped so low that the missionaries traveled inland to the San Joaquin Valley to recruit the Yokuts Indians.

Most Yokuts were unwilling to come to Santa Cruz. Spanish laws forbade priests from forcing Indians to join a mission, but Father Manuel Fernández of Mission Santa Cruz broke these laws. He captured a number of Yokuts and baptized them.

Although untrained as doctors, the missionaries looked after ill neophytes and studied medical books to learn how to help the sick. But European healing methods of the time

Indian men who did not live on mission lands used the temescal, *or sweat lodge (left), to purify their bodies. After a period of heavy sweating, the Indians jumped into a stream to cool off (below). Heavy sweating, however, only worsened the effects of some European diseases.*

were of little use. Thousands of Indians died, especially the very old and the very young. Terrified of sickness, neophytes ran away from Mission Santa Cruz, spreading the diseases to non-mission Indians. Even the medicine of the shamans could not cure European diseases.

Runaways and Punishments

At Santa Cruz, escaped neophytes were a major problem for the Franciscans. Many neophytes ran away to escape illness or poor treatment or to reunite with their families. The neophyte population at Santa Cruz was always among the lowest of California's missions, never topping 523.

Punishment at Mission Santa Cruz was harsh, especially for captured runaways. In fact, the Spaniards whipped neophytes for large and small offenses, such as forgetting prayers, wearing dirty blankets in church, or working too slowly.

The Ohlone at Mission Santa Cruz liked some missionaries but distrusted others for their cruelty. "We were always trembling with fear of the lash," recalled one Santa Cruz neophyte. Some Franciscans punished neophytes by making them wear leg irons or by putting them in prison.

The neophytes at Mission Santa Cruz found ways to protest against the bad treatment. In 1794 Spanish soldiers captured several runaways and sent them to the Presidio of San Francisco for punishment. The non-Christian husband of one of the imprisoned women organized an attack on Mission Santa Cruz. His group injured two guards and burned several mission buildings.

In 1812 Father Andrés Quintana, who was in charge of the mission, ordered severe beatings with a wire-tipped whip for two Santa Cruz neophytes. In revenge, several neophytes strangled Quintana with his own cape. The Franciscans assumed Quintana had died from natural causes. But a few years later, his replacement discovered that Quintana had been murdered. The priest sent those involved to the presidio, where they were found guilty, whipped for nine days, and sentenced to public labor.

Father Ramón Olbés came to Santa Cruz in 1818. Olbés was fitful and nearly insane, possibly because of ill health. "He was very bad and could not be trusted," remembered one Santa Cruz Indian. "Even to the little children of 8 to 10, he would order 25 lashes given at the hand of a strong man, either on the buttocks or the stomach." In protest the Santa Cruz Indians threw roof tiles and stones at him for his cruelty.

Violence, however, wasn't a common form of resistance at Santa Cruz. More often, the Indians reacted to harsh treatment with poorly accomplished work, theft, and refusal to speak Spanish. Some neophytes secretly practiced traditional

Neophytes often tried to escape from Mission Santa Cruz. In 1798 alone, 80 adults and 58 children—nearly one-fourth of the mission's population—fled. About 50 neophytes left in 1809. Ten years later, 104 Yokuts ran away. Indians may have been trying to avoid illness or rough treatment or may have been seeking to return to their villages and families.

The neophytes of Santa Cruz lived in adobe housing that still stands on the mission site.

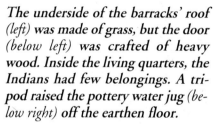

The underside of the barracks' roof (left) was made of grass, but the door (below left) was crafted of heavy wood. Inside the living quarters, the Indians had few belongings. A tripod raised the pottery water jug (below right) off the earthen floor.

Indian ceremonies. Because these rituals weren't part of the Catholic religion, most missionaries didn't approve of them.

More Hard Times

In 1818 the pirate Hippolyte de Bouchard raided Monterey and headed for Mission Santa Cruz. Father Lasuén ordered Father Olbés to take the Santa Cruz neophytes north to Mission Santa Clara for safety.

But Bouchard never landed in Santa Cruz. Instead, while everyone was away, the Californios of Branciforte looted the mission. They slashed grain bags and burned stables, worksheds, and corrals. Mission Santa Cruz was ruined. Upon his return, Father Olbés asked permission to abandon the mission. But Father Lasuén ordered Father Olbés to stay.

Santa Cruz never fully recovered from the attack. In the following years, the neophytes raised more livestock and crops and rebuilt the structures that had been burned. Over time the mission successfully produced cattle hides and tallow (fat used to make soap and candles) for trade. But the neophyte population remained low, and the Indians continued to run away or die from disease.

Mission San Juan Bautista

The Franciscans believed that too many non-Christian Indians lived between Missions Carmel and Santa Cruz. The priests feared that the area wasn't safe for travel. On June 24, 1797, Father Lasuén founded San Juan Bautista to ease the journey between the other two missions. San Juan Bautista, named for Saint John the Baptist, became the fifteenth Franciscan mission in Alta California.

The site of the new mission lay in a broad valley not far from the Pajaro and Salinas rivers. The nearby mountains provided plenty of timber. The area also had a large population of Indians whom the Franciscans could try to recruit. Less than a mile south of San Juan Bautista, for instance, lay the village of Xisca where many Mutsen Ohlone lived.

In spring neophytes at Mission San Juan Bautista marked the newborn calves with this brand.

46

Building the Mission

The Franciscans felt they had chosen a good spot for San Juan Bautista. In fact, it turned into the most productive mission in the Monterey Bay area. San Juan Bautista baptized the most people, grew an abundance of crops, and produced a bounty of goods.

The mission's first priests—Fathers José Manuel Martiarena and Pedro Adriano Martínez—were kind and enthusiastic. Within six months, the priests and neophytes had built a small adobe church,

The Franciscans at San Juan Bautista directed neophyte workers to construct the mission buildings as well as to plow cropland.

47

During the 1800s, the church at San Juan Bautista (above) was remodeled several times. Despite being built in an earthquake-prone area, the mission's arches (facing page, top left) didn't collapse when destructive tremors shook the site. Limestone baptismal fonts (facing page, bottom) held water for baptizing the neophytes. The Indians also carved and painted the mission's furniture (facing page, top right).

priests' quarters, a granary, and neophyte housing. The Franciscans also directed the planting of many crops, including wheat and a variety of vegetables.

From the very start, San Juan seemed to have fewer setbacks than either Carmel or Santa Cruz had experienced. Even when things did go wrong, they sometimes worked out for the better. For example, part of the adobe church collapsed in 1800 during a series of earthquakes. This destructive event encouraged the priests to design a bigger church to accommodate the mission's growing neophyte population.

Between 1803 and 1812, workers labored on the church, which they unknowingly located on the San Andreas Fault (a break in the earth's crust that causes earthquakes along the Pacific coast). The church experienced tremors and several actual quakes but remained standing.

The new church—the largest in Alta California—was one of the most beautiful buildings in the mission chain. Seven huge stone arches lined each side. Workers made the whitewashed walls four feet thick for sturdiness. Neophytes painted floral designs on the church doors and windows.

The inside of the church featured a hand-carved, limestone baptismal font (bowl), which

Father Felipe del Arroyo de la Cuesta enlarged the church at San Juan Bautista.

held the holy water used for baptisms. A wooden statue of Saint John the Baptist adorned the wall behind the altar.

Kindly Priest

Unlike some of the priests at Santa Cruz, San Juan's missionaries were generally more cheerful and productive. Father Felipe del Arroyo de la Cuesta, for example, came to San Juan Bautista in 1808. He helped to complete and equip the huge new church. Father de la Cuesta designed and oversaw the construction of the second and third naves (main halls), which greatly increased the width of the church. His knowledge of design helped to make the building stable even on its shaky ground.

In addition to his design skills, Father de la Cuesta was a good manager, a learned scholar, and a patient teacher. He named many baptized Ohlone children after ancient Greek and Roman writers and leaders, including Alexander, Caesar, Plato, and Cicero. His interest in the Indians' traditional lifeways—unusual among the missionaries—led Father de la Cuesta to study several Ohlone dialects. Eventually, with the help of Mutsen Ohlone women, he compiled a Mutsen Ohlone grammar book with more than 2,800 phrases translated into Spanish.

Musical Interests

Between 1812 and 1815, Spain sent a questionnaire to each mission. The king wanted to know whether the missions had made any progress in converting Indians to the Catholic faith and to Spanish ways. Father de la Cuesta answered the questionnaire with far more detail and sympathy than the fathers from Carmel or Santa Cruz did.

One of the king's questions asked about traditional music. Father de la Cuesta reported that the Ohlone had many tunes and that they varied. "They have songs for their games, different ones for the men and for the women. Other songs they have for funerals, others for healing, still others to scoff at their enemies, for going to war, for the hunt, for the men's and women's dances, for entertaining the youth, and many other stories and fables . . . ." The priest also described the many Indian musical instruments, including whistles, flutes, rattles, and clappers.

In 1815 Father Estéban Tápis, who had recently retired as father-president, joined Father de la Cuesta at San Juan. The two priests shared an interest in studying different subjects. They collected books in Latin, Spanish, French, and Portuguese for

Mutsen Ohlone living at Mission San Juan Bautista helped Father de la Cuesta put together a dictionary of Ohlone words and phrases. Listed below are some common terms and what they mean in English.

akat	shell ornament
am-ani	rain
ana	mother
ap-a	father
arwe	oak tree
mas	beads
raxopa	rays of the sun
suwene	song
ulis	basket
uner	wild onion
uraka	salmon
wasaka	eagle

51

the mission library. The books covered construction, philosophy, theology, geography, music, language, and medicine.

Father Tápis was a creative music instructor. Like most Spanish missionaries, he taught neophyte children to memorize their prayers through songs. But Father Tápis didn't stop there. He also made up a system to teach the neophytes how to read music. He copied the musical notes for chants and hymns onto large pieces of paper. Then the priest arranged musical scores for different ranges in voice. He color-coded each note so choir members could easily follow their parts.

Under Father Tápis's direction, San Juan Bautista's boys' choir became one of the best in Alta California. Choir members

Choir members at San Juan Bautista sang from special hymn books (below left). Father Estéban Tápis led the choir. His grave marker (below) sits near the altar of the mission's church.

The priests at San Juan Bautista taught the neophytes a variety of farming techniques.

also played violins and drums. The choir was so devoted to music that they continued to perform on their own, 40 years after the priest's death.

Although the missionaries at San Juan Bautista tried to be kind and to learn Indian ways, the Franciscans also made the Indians work hard. As at other missions, neophytes at San Juan Bautista constructed buildings, planted and harvested crops, tended livestock, and manufactured goods. But unlike most missions, San Juan Bautista continued to baptize many Indians throughout the 1820s. In 1823, for instance, San Juan's population was at its peak, housing 1,248 neophytes.

PART THREE

Secularization of the Missions

IN 1810 NEW SPAIN BEGAN FIGHTING FOR INDEPEN-
dence from Spain. Straining for money and supplies, Spain stopped
sending ships to the missions. The missionaries and soldiers des-
perately needed goods and began to trade with foreign ships. Spain
was powerless to stop these illegal activities. Instead of money, the
missions bartered cattle hides and tallow for tools, paintings, and
other items.

*An artist's image of Mission Carmel shows Indians, Franciscans, and for-
eigners milling about the compound. By the early 1800s, Spain was no longer
sending supplies to Alta California. By 1821 the empire had lost New Spain
(its colony in North America), which then became the Republic of Mexico.*

In 1815 an additional burden was placed on the missions. New Spain's revolutionary government required them to provide free food and clothing to the soldiers stationed at the presidios. In 1821 New Spain won its war against Spain and became the Republic of Mexico. The new nation claimed Alta California but could not support its missions or presidios. As a result, in 1826 Mexico began taxing each mission 10 percent of its produce to maintain the military forts.

The new tax caused many missions to struggle to keep going. By this time, some of the missions had plenty of cattle but few neophytes. Large numbers of Indians had either died from disease or had run away.

Meanwhile, some people in the new Mexican government believed that the ways of the Spanish missions were outdated. These leaders accused the Franciscans of being harsh and felt that neophytes should be free to leave the missions. In addition, Mexico viewed the missions as too powerful, wealthy, and connected to Spain.

> RICHARD HENRY DANA WROTE OF CARMEL IN THE 1830S, "THE MEN WERE EMPLOYED . . . IN WORKING THE GARDEN, WHICH IS FILLED . . . WITH THE BEST FRUITS OF THE CLIMATE."

Many Californios also felt the missions were too rich. The settlers were jealous that the Franciscans had taken over most of the region's best farming and grazing land. These Californios wanted the land for themselves. To strip all power from the Franciscans and their missions, Mexico decided to close them.

New Laws

In the 1820s and 1830s, Mexico passed a series of laws to take power away from the Franciscans. This process, called secularization, meant that the mission churches would stay open but would be run by secular priests. These priests would not perform missionary work or oversee neophyte laborers but would only serve those who already followed the Catholic faith.

In 1829 Mexico asked Spanish-born missionaries to swear loyalty to Mexico. Most refused and were asked to leave Alta California. But because Mexico did not have enough secular priests to send to the territory, some mission churches were without priests. Several older missionaries, including Father de la Cuesta, stayed and continued to serve their mission.

By the early 1830s, the neophyte populations were declining. About 900 neophytes still lived at San Juan Bautista, compared with 284 at Santa Cruz and 185 at Carmel. Between 1834 and 1836, Mexico passed new laws that ended Franciscan control of the California missions. By this time, the total Indian population throughout the territory had dropped sharply.

In the early 1830s, secularization laws freed the neophytes. The Mexican government required each mission to make a list of its land, livestock, and other holdings. Government-appointed administrators were then supposed to divide up mission property between the ex-neophytes and the Californios. The hope was that the Indians could now support themselves, as the Spaniards had originally planned. By attempting to treat the ex-neophytes fairly, Mexico hoped to prevent the Indians from rebelling against non-Indian settlers.

In 1833 Father-President Narciso Durán greeted José Figueroa, the new Mexican governor of California. Accompanying Figueroa were Mexican priests from Zacatecas, a region in central Mexico.

Mexico eventually appointed civil administrators to oversee the distribution of mission property.

The Franciscans, however, argued that the neophytes were not ready for self-government. The priests had always thought of the Indians as children who needed care and supervision. The missionaries also feared that newcomers would take away mission lands intended for the Indians. Many Californios and Mexicans accused the Franciscans of making excuses so they could still control mission land

and wealth. Despite the views of the priests, secularization continued.

Meanwhile, Mexico's new government was broke from fighting its war for independence. Instead of paying its debts to soldiers and private citizens in cash, Mexico gave them tracts of mission land. Soon these people were running large ranchos on acreages originally meant for ex-neophytes.

Broken Promises

Mexico's new government was largely unstable, and officials weren't able to keep track of the activities of the civil administrators. Instead of giving mission property to the ex-neophytes as planned, many administrators sold land and livestock to their own relatives and friends or simply helped themselves.

The Franciscans watched as most mission land was given to Mexicans and Californios. Ex-

neophytes who did receive land or supplies were often cheated into selling their property at low prices. Many mission Indians were forced to find work at the ranchos, where they hardly earned more than room and board.

For most ex-neophytes, there was no place to go. The old vil-

Secularization laws allowed Indians to leave the missions legally. But once outside the missions, without money or jobs, many ex-neophytes ended up homeless and poor.

lages were gone. Vast areas of native plant foods had been destroyed by domestic animals. Ranchers now occupied land around Monterey Bay that had traditionally belonged to the Ohlone. Hunting and gathering skills had been lost with the deaths of so many Native Americans during mission times. The former neophytes could no longer live according to the old ways.

Some ranchers allowed Indians to establish new villages on ranchland in exchange for working. Other Native Americans drifted back to the missions, where they farmed small plots of land. Still other ex-neophytes fled inland to live with the surviving groups of Indians.

Mission San Carlos Borromeo

At Carmel secularization began in 1834. Within a year, most of the Indians had left. Mission production almost came to a complete stop.

In 1835 U.S. trader Richard Henry Dana visited Carmel. He later wrote a popular book called *Two Years Before the Mast.* In it Dana described his adven-tures trading hides and tallow with ranchers in Monterey and elsewhere along the coast. He also mentioned the ex-neophytes who stayed at Carmel tending gardens and livestock. His account of Alta California became a bestseller in the United States.

Administrators gave land along the Carmel River to some ex-neophytes of Mission San

59

Carlos Borromeo. The family of Juan Onesima got one of the largest tracts. As a boy, Onesima had helped build Carmel's church and had played violin for the choir. On this land, Onesima's family raised corn, tomatoes, and onions to sell in Monterey.

But the Native Americans had a hard time marketing their produce. Most settlers disliked Indians and wouldn't buy goods from them. Ranchers who lived near Juan Onesima resented that a Native American owned fertile land along the river. Out of anger and jealousy, they killed Onesima's son-in-law.

By 1839 only 30 mission Indians remained at Carmel. The priest had moved to Monterey. Soon no one lived in the buildings at Mission San Carlos.

Mission Santa Cruz

Secularization at Santa Cruz also began in 1834. At that time, the

Lorenzo Asisara

Years after secularization, historians wrote down the remembrances of neophytes. The story of Lorenzo Asisara, an Ohlone born in 1820 at Mission Santa Cruz, is taken from interviews recorded in 1877 and 1890:

"[Father Antonio] Reál came when the mission was secularized. I was only 13 or 14 at the time . . . . He said the officials would take everything for themselves, and he was right . . . .

Few [ex-neophytes] received much from the redistribution. [José] Ricardo, the choirmaster, got a small land plot on the northwest side of the [quadrangle]. . . .

In 1838 a smallpox outbreak killed many Santa Cruz Indians. By 1839 there were maybe 70 of us left around the mission.

I lived with José Ricardo . . . until 1866. Then the Americans drove us out. Now we get by doing ranch work and hauling firewood. There are scarcely any of our people left."

Eloisa Rodríguez

This story is about Eloisa Rodríguez. Eloisa was a granddaughter of Roman Rodríguez, a Californio who grew up in Branciforte:

Eloisa was born in 1857 in her grandfather's old adobe house, which was once the Indian barracks at Mission Santa Cruz. Her grandfather was granted two rooms in the barracks in 1839, when an administrator divided the mission. Roman bought a third room from mission Indians.

Eloisa's grandfather received a large sheep ranch that had also been part of the mission. When Eloisa was young, she and her family farmed the old mission lands.

In 1865 the Rodríguez family sold the sheep ranch for a good price and bought more land around Santa Cruz County. Because the Rodríguezes got a paper deed proving ownership, they weren't cheated out of their property like so many of their friends.

mission had 5,000 head of cattle and many sheep, horses, burros, and oxen. Father Antonio Reál managed to give some Indians money and gifts before the administrators could take stock of all the items. But, after the arrival of the civil administrator, the ex-neophytes at Santa Cruz received little of what was rightfully theirs. Instead local ranchers quickly took control of the mission's best grazing and farming lands.

Francisco Soto, the administrator at Santa Cruz in 1839, continued to deny the Indians their promised share of property. He also abused them with blows and kicks. José Bolcoff replaced Soto and gave the remaining land and animals to the ex-neophytes. Bolcoff assigned living and gardening space to several Indian families. Others lived around the quadrangle. Meanwhile, a smallpox epidemic reduced the Native American population at Santa Cruz to 71.

Within a few years, many ex-neophytes had sold their property to local ranchers and had moved on. By 1848 the ex-neophytes had established three *rancherías,* or Indian settlements, beyond the outskirts of Santa Cruz. Here they planted vegetables to sell to non-Indians. But settlers eventually drove the Native Americans away and took over their land.

Mission San Juan Bautista

At San Juan Bautista, secularization took longer than it did at the other two missions around Monterey Bay. A major reason was that few ranchers had settled near the inland mission, causing less competition for land.

The few inland settlers who were there had claimed the best lands. But this left about $8,000 worth of goods, seeds, grain, and tools to be divided among the 63 Indian families still living at the mission. Some of the ex-neophytes received plots of land, but many of the tracts were too poor for successful farming.

Gradually, the ex-neophytes of San Juan headed farther inland. Some settled in Indian Canyon (south of present-day Hollister). To survive many found work at the local ranchos. Some ex-neophytes began raiding ranchos and missions for livestock, food, or revenge.

Statehood

As the mission era came to a close, the first wagon trains full of families from the United States rolled in from the east. Many of these settlers urged the U.S. government to make Alta California part of the United States.

In the spring of 1846, an ambitious U.S. commander named John C. Frémont led an armed force into the territory. When the Mexican governor ordered

During the Mexican War (1846–1848), U.S. naval troops defeated Mexican forces at Monterey. Here, American sailors cheer and salute the raising of the U.S. flag at the presidio.

the troops to leave, Frémont encouraged the area's U.S. settlers to rebel against Mexican rule.

Frémont was not aware, however, that the United States and Mexico were already fighting the Mexican War (1846–1848). In fact, the U.S. Navy had taken over the Presidio of Monterey.

Near San Juan Bautista, rancher José Castro drove out Frémont and his men. But in 1847 the well-armed U.S. military forced the Mexicans to surrender to the United States. At the war's end, Alta California became the U.S. territory of California. By 1850 it had become the thirty-first state of the Union.

The population of the new state swelled, and settlers looked greedily at the vast coastal ranchos held by the Californios. The U.S. government felt that many of the land grants made during secularization were illegal. As a result, all land holders now had to prove ownership by a certain date.

But Spain and Mexico had not always provided Californios with the documents describing their land grants. A handshake and a pledge of honor had traditionally sealed land transfers. Now many ranchers had to

> TO ENCOURAGE U.S. SETTLEMENT OF CALIFORNIA, DANA WROTE, "THE [CALIFORNIOS] ARE . . . IDLE . . . . IN THE HANDS OF AN ENTERPRISING PEOPLE, WHAT A COUNTRY THIS MIGHT BE!"

argue their cases in court. During the court battles, Americans called squatters simply moved onto ranchers' lands. Costly court fees eventually forced many Californios to give up the

fight. Many of them moved to California's southern coastal towns or to Mexico.

Native Americans were never even informed about the new proof-of-ownership ruling. In addition, U.S. law did not allow Indians to testify in court. Because they had no legal way to protect their rights, Native Americans soon lost what little land they had to the Americans.

Without the missions or the ranchos, ex-neophytes had few places to go. The U.S. government then began to establish **reservations**—land set aside for Indians and protected by law from outside settlers. Most reservations were on land too poor for farming or ranching. The Indians had to rely on government supplies to survive.

In the late 1800s, the number of settlers in California continued to grow, threatening Native American communities that still existed inland. Waves of cholera wiped out thousands of Indians.

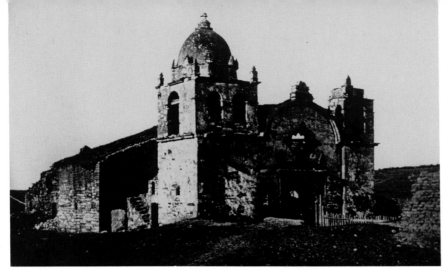

In the late 1800s, the church at Carmel had no roof, and the mission's stone buildings were crumbling.

Settlers shot many more Indians and enslaved their children. The few Native peoples left lived on reservations, worked on farms, did odd jobs, or begged.

By the early 1900s, only about 17,000 Native Americans were living in the state. Many people believed that the Indians of California, including the Ohlone, had died out.

The Missions Crumble

Meanwhile, the missions were falling apart from neglect. People had stolen roof tiles, causing the adobe to rot from exposure to rain. The buildings also crumbled and cracked with almost every earthquake. The U.S. government had returned most mission buildings to the Catholic Church, but the Church had little money to renovate them.

By the 1850s, Mission San Carlos Borromeo was in ruins. The church's roof had caved in. Cattle grazed inside the walls, while squirrels and owls nested in the rafters. Settlers hauled away roof tiles and stone blocks for use in their own construction.

The tower fell off the church at Mission Santa Cruz in 1840. Enough Indian and Mexican churchgoers still lived nearby to rebuild it. But in 1857 an earthquake severely damaged the repaired structure. Townspeople then built a temporary wooden frame church to replace the old adobe one. By 1890 the only original building still standing at the mission was the neophyte barracks.

At San Juan Bautista, priests kept the mission church in good shape. Despite its location on the San Andreas Fault, San Juan Bautista fared better than the churches at Carmel and Santa Cruz.

In 1865 Father Ciprian Rubio drastically changed the appearance of San Juan's church. He installed a New England-style bell tower and steeple. He also covered the tile floors with wooden planks, paneled the adobe walls, and plastered over designs that had been painted on the walls.

The town of San Juan Bautista had grown up around the mission. By the late 1800s, the city had become an important stop for the Coastline Stage, a stagecoach that ran between the larger cities of San Jose and Los Angeles. In addition, ranchers regularly bought horses and cattle in San Juan Bautista and then hired cowboys to drive the herds to San Francisco for sale.

But San Juan Bautista's boom as a stagecoach and ranching town was short lived. In the 1870s, the railroad bypassed the town, turning it back into a quiet corner of the Monterey Bay area.

In 1857 earthquakes led to the collapse of Santa Cruz's church (left). The ceiling caved in, exposing the inside of the structure. The exterior of San Juan Bautista (below) was holding up fairly well in the late 1800s, but an earthquake in 1906 caused severe damage.

PART FOUR

The Missions in Modern Times

IN 1884 A NOVEL CALLED *RAMONA,* BY HELEN HUNT Jackson, hit bookshops throughout the country. Jackson wrote the popular romantic story to show the public how Indians in California had suffered at the hands of U.S. settlers. Instead, readers embraced the book's charming images of life at the early missions and ranchos. Soon afterward, writers and painters featured the old mission architecture in their works.

The British artist Edwin Deakin gave Mission Santa Cruz an abandoned look in his painting from the early 1900s.

Land developers trying to attract settlers used the missions as symbols of romance, hospitality, and healthy, relaxed outdoor living. People began to appreciate the old mission architecture. But, by this time, it was almost too late to save any of the crumbling structures.

Wealthy people soon began organizing groups interested in rebuilding the mission ruins. Charles F. Lummis, a California journalist, was one of the most dedicated. He founded the Landmarks Club to raise money for mission restoration. The club repaired several ruined churches, where visitors could picnic, sketch, and explore.

Restoring San Carlos

Father Angelo Casanova of Monterey also recognized the new public interest in the old missions. In 1879 he began charging a ten-cent admission to Carmel. The money was ear-

Harry Downie used his carpentry skills to repair statues at Carmel and later was in charge of restoring the entire mission.

marked to pay for needed roof repairs. The 100th anniversary of Junípero Serra's death was coming in 1884, and Casanova hoped to replace the roof in time for the celebration.

In nearby Monterey, a large resort hotel called the Del Monte opened. A tourist boom followed, and Father Casanova collected enough donations to reroof in time. The new roof, built in the Gothic style, was completely unlike the original.

Nevertheless, the covering protected the church from further damage for the next 50 years.

In the early 1900s, Father R. M. Mestres, the priest in charge of San Carlos, had collected many early paintings and sketches of the mission quadrangle. But he had no money to start the restoration. In 1914 King Alfonso XIII of Spain sent funds to the Roman Catholic Church to begin the project.

Father Mestres's work was expanded by a skilled cabinetmaker named Harry Downie. In 1931 he began repairing Carmel's chipped statues. He recarved missing limbs, patched broken pieces, and repainted bare spots. The Catholic Church then appointed Downie to restore Carmel's mission church.

Downie wanted Carmel to look exactly as the neophytes had originally built it. He researched carefully, studying old letters, drawings, and photographs. He interviewed people who had lived during secularization. In addition, Downie learned the old methods of woodworking and adobe making.

Downie built a museum on the mission grounds to display paintings and religious items from mission times. Local families and the Monterey Presidio chapel had kept some of these relics since the early 1800s. Downie also managed to gather many of the books collected long ago by Father Serra and Father Lasuén.

In 1945 the Catholic Church opened a private elementary school on the quadrangle's east side. And in 1960, Pope John XXIII (the leader of the Roman Catholic Church) granted the church at Carmel the title of *basilica,* because of its historical importance.

Retiling continues at Mission San Carlos in the 1990s.

Restoring Santa Cruz

The old adobe Indian barracks of Mission Santa Cruz remained in the care of two families. The last family member, Cornelia Rodríguez Hopcroft, died in 1983. The rest of the old mission quadrangle was plowed under for new settlement on what was known as Mission Hill. Holy Cross Church

—a brick structure with high, New–England–style steeples— opened in 1889 on the site of the old mission church. Wooden houses lined the old quadrangle.

In 1931 the Roman Catholic Church built a copy of the first mission church on the quadrangle. The church stands 200 feet south and east of the founding site. A small museum inside displays statues, candlesticks, and paintings once used at Mission Santa Cruz.

In the 1980s, California State Parks and Recreation acquired the Indian barracks—the only original piece of Mission Santa Cruz still standing. In fact, the barracks is the mission chain's only surviving example of original housing. The state hired archaeologists and historians to study the structure for restoration.

Archaeologists carefully measured, drew, photographed, and excavated the inside of the barracks. They lifted the wooden floors and removed layers of plaster that had been added by

Sifting through the Past

Karen Hildebrand, an archaeologist with California State Parks and Recreation, studies what life might have been like at Mission Santa Cruz. This interview was conducted in 1995.

"We've been digging and screening the dirt by the floors of seven rooms once used as neophyte housing. Historical writings say the neophytes ate cooked grains three times a day. By sifting through the floor dirt, we now know they ate traditional foods, too. There are many fish bones, shells, seeds, and small animal bones.

We recently found buried foundations for an older building. The historians can find very little about this older building in the records. Maybe more excavation will give us some clues."

residents over the years. Historians interviewed old-time residents, combed Spanish reports, and studied maps, photos, and sketches to learn more about how neophytes at Santa Cruz had lived long ago.

The archaeologists and historians discovered that the structure had been a 17-room complex built in the early 1820s for Yokuts families from the San Joaquin Valley. The neophytes there had cooked and eaten traditional foods, made shell-bead money, and scratched designs into the plaster of the walls. Each room had included at least one firepit as well as a loft for storage. A single, tiny window overlooked the gardens. A low doorway opened toward the quadrangle. The rooms were cold, dark, and damp.

After the study was completed, restoration began. Workers reinstalled portals, or long porches, along the front and back of the building. New

Students gather in front of Mission San Juan Bautista, whose unique features include animal tracks baked into the clay floor tiles (inset).

adobe walls replaced the old. Following the original foundations, each of the new rooms measured about 16 by 20 feet.

The barracks is now part of Santa Cruz Mission State Historic Park and is open to visitors. The restorers decorated different rooms to represent specific time periods. The room from the mission period includes storage baskets, food grinding utensils, and beds. The early statehood room features

floral wallpaper and family furnishings from the mid-1800s. Other rooms show archaeological work in progress.

Restoring San Juan Bautista

The church at San Juan Bautista also changed dramatically in the late 1800s. During the remodeling of San Juan Bautista, however, no one made an effort to restore the mission's original

Tony Corona, a descendant of San Juan mission Indians, holds a picture of one of his Ohlone ancestors.

look. Instead builders added a tower and steeple and made other changes to suit the styles of the day.

In 1906 a major earthquake struck the city of San Francisco. The tremors, which were caused by the San Andreas Fault, toppled the outer walls and damaged the interior of the church at San Juan Bautista.

In 1949 Harry Downie, with the same care he had used at Carmel, researched and supervised San Juan's restoration. Workers tore down the tower and patched and replastered the walls. Years later, Downie reinforced the church's side arches.

Historians working at San Juan recently uncovered the church's original painted deco-

rations beneath layers of whitewash. Neophytes had made brilliant paints from crushed minerals and plants to draw flowers and geometric designs. Using similar materials, art historians have touched up or even redone many of the wall decorations in the original style.

In other buildings along the quadrangle, historians have continuously turned up items such as furniture and musical instruments from the past. Researchers have found cooking utensils, grinding tools, and beads. A museum in the restored buildings displays many of these items once used by missionaries and neophytes.

Many people still visit San Juan Bautista, either as church-goers or tourists. The church is the site of many weddings, baptisms, and community events. In fact, every year a local Hispanic theater group—El Teatro Campesino—stages popular traditional Christmas plays in the old mission church.

The Ohlone Today

While the mission buildings regained some of their vigor, Indian groups struggled to keep their cultures alive. During the early 1900s, Ohlone descendants of mission Indians kept in contact with one another.

Although outsiders believed the Ohlone no longer had a shared set of traditions, researchers who interviewed Ohlone were able to collect information about the old languages and customs.

In the 1960s, minorities across the nation began fighting for equal rights and fair treat-

Modern Ohlone work to preserve their culture. Here, an Ohlone man crafts a split-stick clapper, an instrument that accompanies traditional dancing.

ment. Many Native Americans, including the Ohlone, publicly expressed their pride in their heritage. They also wanted equal opportunities for education, jobs, housing, and health care.

Despite years of hardship, the Monterey Bay Ohlone peoples remain proud and unbeaten. They have formed councils such as the Pajaro Valley Ohlone Indian Council of Watsonville, the Amah-Mutsen of Gilroy and San Juan Bautista, and the Carmel Band of Rumsien in Monterey.

Even though Ohlone peoples still survive, the U.S. government does not consider the Ohlone to be an existing tribe. The Ohlone councils are currently seeking recognition by the U.S. government. They want to receive some of the benefits given to other Native Americans in the United States—including the return of a landbase from which they can preserve Ohlone tradition and language.

AFTERWORD

Each year thousands of tourists and students visit the California missions. Many of these visitors look around and conclude that the missions are the same today as they were long ago. But, over time, the missions have gone through many changes. The earliest structures were replaced by sturdier buildings with tall towers and long arcades. But even these solid buildings eventually fell into ruin and later were reconstructed.

Our understanding of the missions also has changed through the years. Missionaries, visitors, novelists, and scholars have expressed different opinions about the California missions. These observers often have disagreed about the impact of the missions on the Indians in California. And the voices of Native Americans—from the past *and* the present—have continued to shed light on the mission experience.

The early Franciscan missionaries believed that they were improving the local Indians by introducing them to mission life. But visitors from Europe and the United States frequently described the Spanish missions as cruel places. A French explorer in 1786, for example, reported that the priests treated the neophytes like slaves. He was horrified that Spanish soldiers tracked down runaway Indians and whipped them for trying to return to their old way of life.

Many early visitors were truly concerned about the mistreatment of Native Americans. But the foreign travelers, jealous of Spain's hold on Alta California, also criticized the missions as a way to prove that Spain wasn't worthy to possess the region. Similarly, a young man from the eastern United States, visiting Alta California in the 1830s, was saddened to see so much sickness and death at the missions. He advised his fellow Americans that the region would fare much better as a part of the United States.

The missions were all but forgotten during the 25 years following the U.S. takeover of California. The once solid structures decayed into piles of rotting adobe. One U.S. visitor wrote that she doubted if any structure on earth was "colder, barer, uglier, [or] dirtier" than a California mission.

Just when the missions had disappeared almost completely, they came roaring back to public attention. Beginning in the 1880s, dozens of novels and plays about early California described the Franciscan priests as kind-hearted souls who treated neophytes with gentleness and care. This favorable image of the missions became popular because it gave many Californians a positive sense of their own history and identity. The writings also attracted droves of tourists to California. Merchants and business leaders in the state supported the rebuilding of the crumbling missions because it made good business sense.

The missions today are still the subject of a lively debate. Some people continue to believe that the missions brought many benefits to the Indians by "uplifting" them to European ways. But many others, including some descendants of the neophytes, say that the missions destroyed Native American lifeways and killed thousands of Indians. For all of us, the missions continue to stand as reminders of a difficult and painful time in California history.

Dr. James J. Rawls
Diablo Valley College

CHRONOLOGY

Important Dates in the History of the Missions of the Monterey Bay Area

1602   Sebastián Vizcaíno maps Monterey Bay

1770   San Carlos Borromeo de Carmelo is founded; Presidio of Monterey is built

1784   Father Junípero Serra dies; Father Fermín Francisco de Lasuén becomes the new father-president

1786   La Pérouse studies the Monterey Bay area

1791   Santa Cruz is founded; Malaspina visits Carmel

1793   Vancouver stays at Mission San Carlos; Manuel Ruíz draws plans for Carmel's church

1797   San Juan Bautista is founded; Branciforte is established near Santa Cruz

1810   Revolution begins in New Spain

1818   Hippolyte de Bouchard raids Monterey

1821   New Spain gains independence from Spain

1830s   Missions are secularized

1846   Mexican War begins; U.S. Navy occupies Monterey

1848   Mexican War ends; Mexico cedes Alta California to the United States

1850   California becomes the thirty-first state

1850s   U.S. government begins to return the California missions to the Catholic Church; mission buildings are falling apart

1890s–present   Missions are restored

ACKNOWLEDGMENTS

Photos, maps, and artworks are used courtesy of: Laura Westlund, pp. 1, 13, 19, 30, 33, 38, 40, 46; © Diana Petersen, pp. 2, 18 (left and right), 20, 24 (right), 28, 49 (top right and bottom), 52 (right), 71 (inset), 72; Southwest Museum, Los Angeles, CA, pp. 8–9 (photo by Don Meyer, CT. 374-646.G136); North Wind Picture Archives, p. 10; © Betty Crowell, p. 12; © Shirley Jordan, pp. 15, 45 (bottom left), 49 (top left), 52 (left); © John Elk III, pp. 16, 34 (bottom), 50, 71; © Frank Balthis, p. 16 (top inset); Sherry Shahan, pp. 16 (bottom inset), 31; © Eda Rogers, p. 18 (middle); © Chuck Place, pp. 21, 34 (top left); Independent Picture Service, pp. 27, 47, 53, 57, 58 (left), 59, 62, 74–75 (photo by Nancy Smedstad); Museum of New Mexico, pp. 22 (right), 37, 54, 64; © Jo Ann Ordano, pp. 23, 73; San Juan Bautista State Historical Park, pp. 24 (left), 25; Library of Congress, p. 32; © Richard R. Hansen, p. 34 (top right); Bancroft Library, pp. 22 (left), 36, 39, 41 (top), 42 (right); Dept. of Lib. Services, Am. Museum of Natural History, p. 41 (bottom); CA Historical Society, Title Insurance & Trust Photo Coll., Dept. of Special Coll., USC Library, pp. 42 (left), 65 (left); © Galyn C. Hammond, p. 44; © Yamada-Lapides Photography, pp. 45 (top and bottom right); © Don Eastman, p. 48; Dept. of Special Coll., Univ. of CA at Santa Cruz, p. 58 (right); San Juan Bautista Historical Society, p. 65 (bottom); Seaver Center for Western History Research, Natural History Museum of Los Angeles County, p. 67; Pat Hathaway Coll. of California Views, p. 68; © Diane C. Lyell, p. 69; Emily Abbink, p. 80 (top); Dr. James J. Rawls, p. 80 (middle); Professor Edward D. Castillo, p. 80 (bottom). Cover: (Front) © Galyn C. Hammond; (Back) Laura Westlund.

Quotations are from the original or translated writings or statements of Jean-François de Galaup, Count of La Pérouse, pp. 35, 37; unnamed Santa Cruz neophyte, p. 43; Father Felipe del Arroyo de la Cuesta, p. 51; Richard Henry Dana, pp. 56, 63; Lorenzo Asisara, p. 60; Karen Hildebrand, p. 70.

METRIC CONVERSION CHART

WHEN YOU KNOW	MULTIPLY BY	TO FIND
inches	2.54	centimeters
feet	0.3048	meters
miles	1.609	kilometers
square feet	0.0929	square meters
acres	0.4047	hectares
ounces	28.3495	grams
pounds	0.454	kilograms
gallons	3.7854	liters

INDEX

acorns, 18, 20, 21
adobe, 32, 38, 39, 44–45, 61, 64–65, 69, 71, 75
agriculture and livestock, 12, 14–15, 20, 32, 35, 39, 40, 47, 53, 56; cattle brands, 30, 38, 46. *See also* ranchos
Alta California, 12, 14–15, 30, 31, 56; becoming a state, 62–63; European exploration of, 25–27, 35–38; first peoples of, 8, 17–25. *See also* California
animals, 16–17, 18–19, 22
architecture, 4, 32–34, 37–38, 39, 44–45, 47–50, 68–73
Asisara, Lorenzo, 60

Baja California, 11, 12. *See also* Mexico; New Spain
baptism, 8, 31, 32, 41, 47, 48–50, 53
Bolcoff, José, 61
Bouchard, Hippolyte de, 45–46
Branciforte, 40, 46, 61

Cabrillo, Juan Rodríguez, 25
California, 63–64, 67–68, 70, 74–75. *See also* Alta California
Californios, 40, 46, 56, 57, 58, 63
Carmel. *See* San Carlos Borromeo de Carmelo
Casanova, Father Angelo, 68
Catholic Church. *See* Roman Catholic Church
Catholicism. *See* Roman Catholic faith
Cuesta, Father Felipe del Arroyo de la, 50–51, 56

Dana, Richard Henry, 56, 59, 63

diseases, 9, 14, 41–42, 46, 61, 63, 75
Downie, Harry, 68, 69, 72

earthquakes, 48, 64–65, 72
El Camino Reál, 11, 30
exploration, European, 25–27, 35–38, 74

Fernández, Father Manuel, 41
food, 35, 70–71
Franciscan religious order, 12, 14–15, 26, 31, 50–53, 74–75; under secularization laws, 56–58
Frémont, John C., 62–63

Galaup, Jean-François de. *See* La Pérouse

Hildebrand, Karen, 70

Indians. *See* Ohlone; Yokuts

Jackson, Helen Hunt, 67

Landmarks Club, 68
languages, 12, 20, 37, 50–52
La Pérouse, 35–37
Lasuén, Father Fermín Francisco de, 35, 38, 45–46
Lummis, Charles F., 68

Malaspina, Alejandro, 37
Mestres, Father R. M., 68–69
Mexico, 15, 55, 56–58, 62–63. *See also* Baja California; New Spain

missions: fight for control over, 56–59; founding of, 11, 26, 31; goals of, 11–12, 26, 31; life at, 14, 15, 32–38, 40–46, 50–53, 54–55, 70–71; methods of obtaining converts for, 12, 30, 32, 35, 39, 41; secularization and its effects on, 15, 56–65, 74–75
Monterey Bay, 15, 16–19, 25, 26–27. *See also* Monterey, Presidio of
Monterey, Presidio of, 27, 30, 38, 39, 62–63, 69
Mutsen Ohlone, 46, 50–51

Native Americans. *See* Ohlone; Yokuts
neophytes: definition of, 12, 32; freeing of, 15, 57. *See also* Ohlone; Yokuts
New Spain, 11, 15, 26, 38, 55–56. *See also* Baja California; Mexico

Ohlone: chiefs of, 20; clothes of, 22; food of, 8, 12, 17, 19, 20, 21, 22; homes of, 22, 23; hunting and fishing, 20, 22, 23; mission life of, 14, 15, 32–38, 40–46, 50–53, 54–55, 70–71; music, 51–52; post-secularization way of life, 9, 15, 58–64, 73; pre-contact way of life of, 8, 17–25; religious ceremonies of, 8, 20, 23–24, 44–45; shamans, 24–25, 42; trade, 20, 23; tribelets, 19–20, 23. *See also* Mutsen Ohlone; Rumsien Ohlone
Olbés, Father Ramón, 43–44, 45–46
Onesima, Juan, 60